'the'
me too
movement

charna ainsworth

'the'

charna ainsworth

Dedication

This collection of poetry is dedicated to you.
The you found in these words.

Contents

Complete

When time collides
within the wall of prayers
the door will open up;
I'll be standing there,
and it'll be me...
that holds *'the'* key
to begin the rest of my life.
It won't be filled
with your tone
saying everything about me
is wrong,
your eyes will never
look at me
the way they do now.
I'll feel complete
for the first time,
without your judgment
upon me.
Yes, after I turn *'the'* key
I'll be free...
         ...forever.

Enough

Within the shield
behind the guard
placed over my heart
a girl who's alive
one not frightened to try
hides silently inside
waiting for her time
to speak the truth
traveling the world
just to protect little girls
from the brutal men
in this unjust world.

All Eternity

The space invaded
by your words
nothing but lies
is shaped by your hatred
darkened by your goodbye
seeking shelter
turned away
for lack of pride
I wanted
I needed,
given my all -
filled by your lies -
fallen into mediocrity -

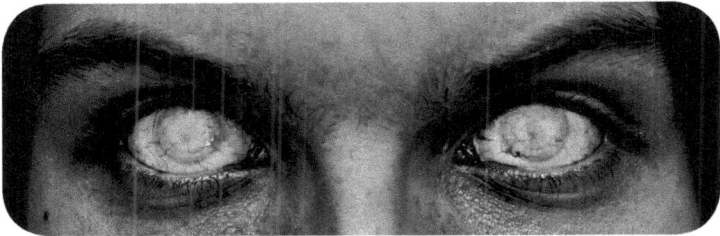

rendered blind;
nothing really matters
this life will soon be over;

your crimes will live on forever.

Pushed

taken with hope
you might just care
show me kindness
just be there
when I'm needing
a shoulder
a friend

how I wish
it were true,
now I know
about you,
the sadness
of your face
looking down on
me
with pity

with distaste…
cruel to say the least
sad to know
the truth;
you're a liar
and a thief,
I no longer
want anything
to do with
someone like you.

Prying Eyes

she was the last of her kind
drifting slowly out to sea
nothing behind
could stop her
the vision was clearly
beyond the reach
of the place
she once called home,
empty and barren
she left all alone
in search of a life
to call her own
without any judgment
of evil
or prying eyes
to witness mistakes
and little white lies,
they all turned to grey
when she walked away
from the life she knew before,
it was easy to say goodbye,
only one tear
left her beautiful eyes
as the boat left the shore...
never to return.

Could Have

He was wrong about me
his words were all lies
sad to say it took many years from me
to understand why he felt the need
to keep me down,
what sadness to think of what might have been

if he'd held me up… cherished my love,
brought out the best in me
instead of feeling like
he'd been given my love
only to break me down
to make him feel high
to squash my dreams…
instead of watching me fly.

Tunnel Vision

There are things I said
lingering in your heart
words to empower
giving life when remembered.
It was simple then
to believe the impossible,
definition of dreamer -
not knowing the obstacles
that soon liter the path
too many obligations>
look at the fingers in the pie,
why should we strive another
moment

letting go, we could release the lie
that bargains with souls
stealing their dreams
until they find themselves old
and it's too late
for what might have been…
what could have been…
if they had never given up.

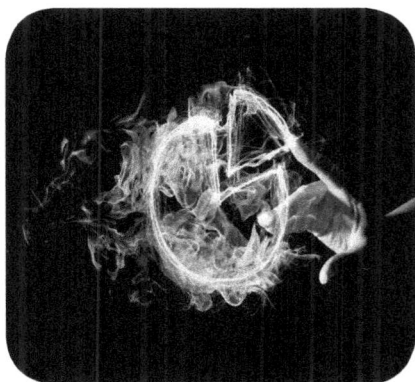

Chasing the Light

straggling the center
opposite the ends
of instruction
and correction
where fool's follow
chasing the light
that beckons…
it calls
promising more
than anyone could define:
keeps the man
lingering in the room;
women stay seated
afraid to appear eager
of a chance
life can be bigger
than food stamps
and HUD housing.
raging rivers
of goodness
drown simple men
while others
wade bravely
turning sorrow to gold
as water rushes by…

Shut

I can only imagine
the monumental complaints
of how I took up space,

wasted oxygen…
while sitting alone
in a tiny dark bedroom
at the end of a trailer.
How I tried so hard
to stay out of sight
to grow smaller with time,
to breathe less…
but of course,
it was no use
I couldn't do anything
right
so I kept my mouth
shut tight
dreaming of my future life
in silence.

Cleansed

Falling past a thousand chances
to not live another day
with your horrid hate;
hoping, wishing, praying
you'll find a way
to tame your demons,
forcing your mind to think straight,
leaving the past behind
with all its mistakes,
embracing the future…
even find love for today,
it could shatter
all the harsh words
and wash away the pain
before I'm certain
to run far, far away.

Calm

trouble
oh, my soul has tasted trouble
found it bitter
spat out the worst
took off running
perpetually in search of peace,
oh, sweet peace

that comes from quiet within
        …a soul
knowing it's worth
refusing to give in or give up
the serenity it's known
for days   -   for months
for weeks   -   for minutes,   or hours
when troUble let it be,
yes, in that time
feeling completely free… from care.

Never Say Goodbye

it was the only way to say goodbye
turn the hope into fear
running with vigor
leaving with might
erasing the memory of you
from every aspect of the life
dreamed about for eternity
to fill the days
accepting every single part
of what they call your soul
becoming too close
losing control
until where I began
and where you end
blurred beyond reason
no one else could comprehend
the depths
I would have gone
to never say goodbye
to the only person on earth
who made me truly feel alive

No One… That's Who

Failure to mature
To reach full potential
Living under the standard
Set before me
When I was little,
Blistering cold
The way the winds blows
Through an empty life
When you have
No one to hold
Accountable for what's been done
Or who could listen
To what's been said
In order for
Something as simple
And complex
As this person's life
To go unread
Is the saddest story
That's ever been written,
Now there…
Feel better…
It's been said.

Directions

Follow your heart wherever it may lead
it's within the darkest hour
the light...

you can plainly see.
When you must decide
between right and wrong,
let there be no hesitation
of what the answer should be.
I've given you skills
and enough love to fill an empty sea...
now go live your life
and remember
whatever is to be... will be.

Searching for Forever

Crystal eyes of love
staring at the ceiling
as arms cradle
souls unite,
why…
so far away
in your head
in your thoughts
searching for forgiveness
in order to give
your all.
Will it be found
in such large amount?
These ugly deeds
are mounting
up to goodbye.
Forgive?
Most certainly.
Live a lie?
Not on your life.

All Your Weight

Within the womb
of hatred and regret

poisoned by cigarettes
and thoughts of
why
ruining your perfect life
before taking
a first breath
was a lot to lay
on a perfect soul
unblemished
by your truth
of never wanting
of never needing
me.

Results…

No more diving deep
memory serves
keeping altered hearts
in the shallows
where it hurts less
than it should.
The irony of it all
is the fear
that only exists
in the aftermath
of this terrible mess.

Searching for Change

blue highway
built on lies
covered in schemes
of making more than we ever seen
in our simple lives
of trailer park rules and childhood games

always searching for change
to escape the past where nothing could last;
it was all broken,
nothing smooth about it,
still we rode…
what else did we know but to ride it out,
bumpy or not,
it was a one-way… one way or another
we would burn that path right into a future
that didn't in any way resemble the tainted past

Out of My Control

My hunger speaks of a distant day
when love was ripped away
from the depths of a little girl's soul.
I was crying as I clung...   to the only one who would run
if I needed anything at all.

The tragedy struck deep
...to the point I would never speak,
with the same voice, ever again.

Beginnings

blood like water
wearing away imperfections
eroding all roughness
evading the soul
the heart of everything
given at birth
beautiful
no question
destined to persevere
reaching heights beyond imagination
without your hate
despite your crimes
no longer lying in wait
of the best;
simply walking away
from what's left of I love yous

Faithless

Words spoken over me
for harm
for good
etch so deeply
in my soul

bringing pain
bringing joy
building my faith
to crash again
at the mention
of your name.
Why do you speak
such mean things
over me?...
- when at this moment
I am
the one and only person

you have
in this world
who still believes
in you....

Speak

There...
pressed against the paper
in my mind's eye
I see the future
full of potential
ripe with rewards
for labor so deep
week after week
of pen and of paper
collecting the life
right out of my mind
fueling the next readers
with precious resource
uncommon to as many
who discovered their voice
    and use it.

Dying Wish

He was sitting comfortably,
when I spoke up and asked…
what is your dying wish?
A quiet voice that trembled and swayed
answered in the twilight…
at the end of day
I've never wanted much
all my life… you see
I was happy for the good ole'
days,
sad to see them leave…
and there was magic
in the sadness
that's hard to describe
kinda like that feeling
when you're standing on the peak
of that mountain you just climbed,
but if I could ask for anything
before I pass on from this life
it would be one more day
with my children and wife.
One of the good ones
full of sunshine
when we were together,
our bodies full of laughter
our hearts full of love.

I moved a little closer
when I saw the twinkle in his eyes
he smiled as best he could
while I thought of a reply.
I'll go get them,
just tell me where they are
it doesn't matter how near
or how far,
I will find them
and I'll bring them to you;
it's your dying wish
it's the least I could do.
He cleared his throat,
the twinkle left his eyes
he stuttered at first
over the words in his mind.
I had two daughters and a son
and one beautiful wife
she passed away
about a decade ago;
I lose track of time.
My son went off to war
came home in a wooden box;
it broke my wife's will to live,
which in turn, broke my heart.
My firstborn daughter...
she's out in the world,
probably doing good.

It's been years since we spoke;
she always thought, I was no good.
You see,
her husband's family
made a lot of money in oil
and her old father
never measured up.
My baby girl's been gone the longest,
we lost her when she was twelve.
It was a hit-and-run.
People always talked
like it was her fault,
said she shouldn't have been
riding her bike after dark.
So… you see young lady…
my wish,
it's impossible to fulfill
unless…
I fall asleep and dream
escaping back into the memory
of one perfect peaceful
spring day in May.

Capturing Moments

Talent can't be learned
only sharpened like a knife
against a smooth stone;
my stone is called life.
Once when I was little
I found a magic pen,
it loved white paper,
it became my cherished friend.
The letters did fall
in perfect array
speaking of the wisdom
to release me from the past.
So... I grew
as the words compiled into memories;
capturing moments,
preserving for all,
a glimpse of talent,
sharpened by time
and life's smooth stone
combined with a never-ending rhyme.

Prediction

you can't see
what I've been through
by looking at me
it's been uphill
-both ways-
most of my life;
funny
what was meant to destroy
strengthen me beyond scope
of what the critics
predicted
of what the haters said
but there is no one
to be proud
of where I am
rising above
where I come from
except me;
for the first time
that's enough.

Breathtaking

I am the author of my life.
I get to write the story.
Each word
I choose on purpose.

Every scene has a reason.
The story I tell is not perfect.
Sometimes, it's a rewrite.
Sometimes, just an edit…
but every once-in-a-while;
it's simply breathtaking.
I close my eyes
savoring it -
the moment
I wrote… only in my mind
now played,
fleshed out… called my life.

If I Follow

There's a force that's invisible
lifting me into the light
giving me purpose and meaning
showing me exactly what's right
for my life.
The path
I must take
in order to fulfill
the mission God gave -
and if I follow…
if I succeed…
you can lay me to rest,
and please…
don't forget
to remember me.

The Hills

Days pass
blurring reason
pursuing purpose
in the hours
in the days
I have yet to live
wanting to fulfill
to be beloved.
Humans are lost,
look at the eyes
that disapprove
and every time
I die a little more.
There is only one,
the one on high
who knows my heart,
His love
is enough,
His strength
is sufficient,
I'll keep
traveling on
until the day
I'm finally home.

Façade

Religion has failed
as miserably as
misery can be
to be an answer,
a final solution
of what's ailing me.
Their fake love
given as a gesture
to prove their love for You
is dry; it's cold
and it will never do.
Anything to heal
the scars that just won't heal…
their fakeness can't reach
into my real.
Now that I think of it,
it's the epitome of oil and water.

You

Wonder
beyond all measure
Proof
love still exists
Reason
to not merely drift
through these days
called life.
When the purpose waivers
and the pollution comes in
your smile
fills me up
keeps me afloat
just enough
to carry on
giving strength to hold

this pen
and capture the moment
no longer held within
a heart too guarded
to share the truth;
That's you.

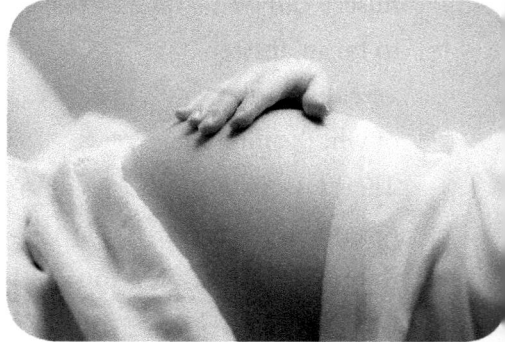

Dreamer

There is no way I'm giving up
no, I'm not backing down
I've been on this ride before
I'm no stranger to this town
see, I've been searching
all my life
for a dream that's going to come true
and nothing and no one
is going to stop me;
I'll never quit until
I break-through
and my reality
becomes the vision
I hold in my mind,
no more holding back
I'll keep on grinding
until I possess
this dream of mine.

Soul's Core

When the storyteller
fails to deliver
a juicy tale
full of love and hate
what will be his fate?...

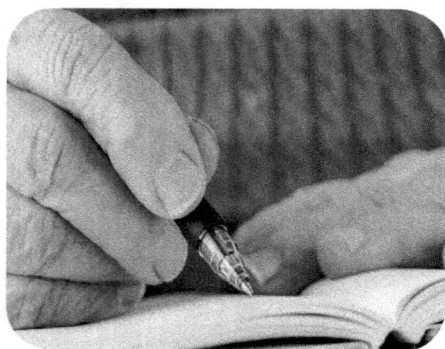

in a world
driven by the lust
of more and more and
more.
Will he be loved
for all the words written,
all the poems freely
given?
Can anyone appreciate

the continual saCrifice
displayed upon the page
as his soul gave and gave?
When his world is at an end
will you read his words once again

finding new meaning, wisdom and truth?
He gave them all to you
without remorse or regret
revealing his soul's core
until the very end.

Daisy

Pretty girl
all in white

you looked at me
and I knew
we were meant to be

still, you looked so sad…
the unchosen
in a crowded room

no one wanted you

but I could see
past your scars and scabs

see who you could be
with love

a beautiful Daisy
to brighten our world.

#rescuedog

Possibilities

there was a whisper on the wind
leading me time and again
to your door,
it was there I found a friend
who understood where I'd been
and cared enough
to show me there's more,
with time I stood up
and bent to my knees
it was then my friend
helped me find me,
it became so clear
I was meant for so much more
than I ever thought possible
before I walked through his door
now every day is better
I was blessed by knowing this man
glad I listened to the whisper
because meeting him was part of the plan

Emerald Coast

Taste the salty sea
from your breath
wave hello to the sun
let toes dance
upon grains of quartz
give your body and soul
a chance to become one
with the shore
with the sand
with the water; so blue
in that moment
you'll understand
all this paradise
has to offer you.

What Is Wrong

If I live another day
I'll search for ways
to get things right
inside my head
inside my mind
where carousels and
rocket ships
go round and up
never crashing down;
no, I'd be high
above what is wrong
with music and laughter
and unbelievable faith
that would make me stronger
than any of the previous days
I've spent
marking off my to-do list…
if I live another day.

You and I

when time rushes by
in a perpetual race
of to-dos
and don'ts
just remember my face
the way we used to laugh
it was our personal song
our souls private dance
no one else was invited
how I miss those days
sometimes, I find myself
longing for times…
when you and I smiled
and shared a warm embrace

Poet's Heart

I will not be ignored
you will remember my name
my words will live on
many years after I'm gone
they will find my books
on a dusty shelf
read them out loud
discussing what they
think the words meant
to a girl like me
on the day I wrote them
down
but their true meanings
will be forever hidden
buried with the girl
brave enough
to share her poet's heart
with the world.

A Moment

Wind blows gently
Owl sings his song
Thomas meows
Stretching out his arms
The chimes play a melody
A red cow eats grass
There's a voice in the distance
The dog stops to scratch
A poet searches for words
To write down
Hoping they will forever last
An alarm reminds her
Time is moving fast
Like a river
Not far from the front porch
All the water flows south
And the words; they flow
In every direction
To and fro
Until the end of life
As *the* poet knows it.

Attempted

Carried by your whim
into an angry night,
blindly trusting
you with my life.
A split-second decision,

jealousy driving you mad.
Packing what little we had
while begging not to go.
As daylight turned to darkness,
no forethought in your plan
…left us
stranded between mountains.
Strong winds
blew foreign snow
with passion and force.
The car stalls

in the darkness
of white out.
Unprepared teenagers
trying to escape death
give their last dollar
to a tow-truck driver.
Just an angel in disguise
one November night
on Laramie's pass.

ffffeee

Choiceless

Saving up the vile
for when we're alone
pouring it out
upon my soul
I'm weak
always weak
wanting it to work
still trapped
in the fairy tale lie
that God sent you
only, the God I knew
would never send
someone like you…
unbalanced and rude,
stealing my truth
with hatred and lies
leaving me no other choice
than to say goodbye.

That Was Yesterday

Who is going to have my back
when it's all said and done?
It's too easy
for you to walk away,
forget that we shared love
forget the words you'd say…
yet I still remember
every single one.
Especially the words
when you're discouraged
reminding me of
what you once had
and how I've let you down
time and time again.
Still, the one thing I wonder,
which will soon be your regret;
is when did it become
my fault
you don't have a perfect life
with a silver platter under it?

Wanting a Friend

when the walls are set
tall and wide and strong
no one can climb over
no one can break through
unless I choose to let them in,
it's defense at its finest
a prayer and a wish
hoping to divert disaster
remembering the pain of before
on the days
when I left the door...

open
wanting a friend
needing someone to care
without a dagger in their hand
or a lie on their lips

What Didn't Kill Me

Whispers and stares
follow my back
as I walked cautiously
through the crowd
of people who know
I'm no longer their prey
or hidden away
from their eyes.
Now I'm wide open,
healed from the pain.
The words they threw
to make them feel big
only made me better...
     made me stronger
so I could live
a life to be proud of
where I no longer hide;
I'm completely me,
Yes, and finally happy.

the depths

Alone in a crowd
you sought me out
to fill the void
inside the depths
of your heart.
Now I wonder
what did you see
the first night
you laid eyes on me?
Within our embrace
I found my place
in the endless world
of relentless strangers.
By the rising sun
my life had become
a matter of finding
my way back to
your sweet embrace.

While You Are Here

Golden light
falling from heaven
embrace your path
ordained before time
watch the sky open wide
with one word,
       one thought
of goodness and happiness
suffer not at anger
it is useless
wasting precious energy
better spent
on laughter and forgiveness
it's the place
you are predestined to live
why you are here
such gifts to give
remember it's freeing
to love more than hate
and maybe the only way
your soul will feel safe
and sheltered from this place.

charna ainsworth

me too

their
time
is
up

charna ainsworth

"She lived as we all have lived, too many years in a culture broken by brutally powerful men. For too long, women have not been heard or believed if they dare speak the truth to the power of those men. But their time is up. Their time is up."

—Oprah Winfrey
Golden Globe Awards
the speech which inspired this book

Dedication

To all the boys and men
who thought they could
destroy the light God put
in my soul, turning it to darkness:
You all failed.

Dedication II

To all the girls and women
who read the pages
of this book
and see yourself in the words:

Don't let them dim your light.
Stop it now…
so you won't have to say,
'Me Too'.
Together, women are
changing the world.
The era in which
brutally powerful men
control our lives
and our decisions is over.
Their time is up!

Beauty for Ashes

contents

the loss of innocence

What happened to me
when I was young?
Many years later
I'm still searching
for a way
to fill the holes
left in my soul
by brutally powerful men.

young and innocent;
door locked
panties down
I became your prey
begging anyone would come
break down the door and save
but she just walked away
at the assurance of your voice
that everything was okay
but I wasn't
and never would be again…

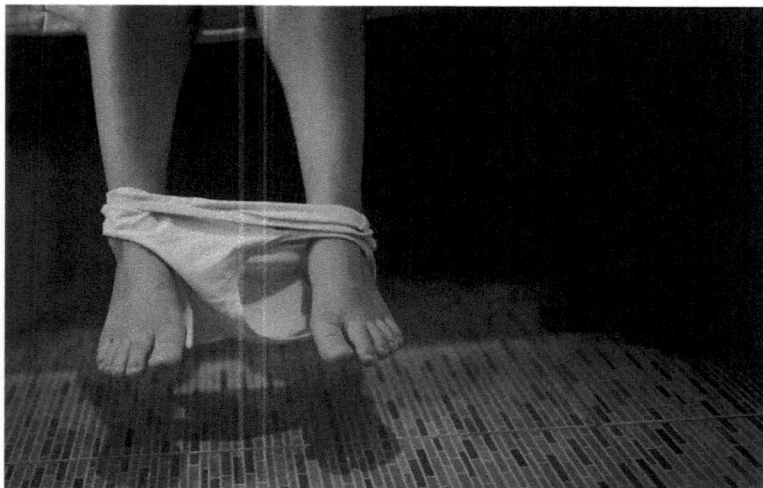

Chased; caught somewhere between
the kitchen and dining room floor.
Pinned; unable to move.
Terrorized, like in pitch darkness.
Daylight streaming through a small window.

Seeing the knife; swallowing the threats-
coming from an unknown voice.
Feeling my soul separate
from a body in jeopardy...
of never being the same.
I stand outside of myself
watching you control; manipulating your claim,
harnessing my power...
for your purpose, for your gain.
The little girl will never be the same.
She'll never be the same!

The old house becomes my prison
as you barricade the doors,
while the adults are off
having a good time,
ditching their chores.
I become a prisoner;
a play thing for you
and your friends.
What else is there to do
besides torture the one
who admires you so...
would do anything...
to be accepted,
would try anything
to mend the fence she never broke.

My flesh didn't belong
    in your hands,
touched by your mouth
discarded for the next victim
    before daylight.
Now, only the secrets remain
buried so deep
    in a *poets* brain;
only words
hint at the pain.

Birth of a poet...

white as fresh snow
my heart and mind open
to all that is good and right
man could have been kind
should have watched me shine
instead of stealing the joy
the very light that was mine

She's thirsty
longing for relief
that comes from
his embrace
but he's a
thousand miles away
holding another girl
who barely knows
his true story
his true soul
the ugly lies he told
his murderous heart
that promised to care
promised to be there
to shelter
to protect
from the brutally
powerful men
who seek
who search
to destroy
the heart
and soul
of his little girl.

little girls go to libraries
to read; to learn
innocently they wander
to books appropriate for their age
trusting that they're safe
(*but they are never safe*)
little girls search
the shelves, up and down
to find the book
the one they like
believing they can read in safety
(*but they are never safe*)
little girls sit down
in overstuffed bean bags
eyes all over the cover
then open up to the
first page, forgetting their safety
(*but they are never safe*)
little girls sit quietly reading
page seven, eight or nine
until they notice the man
out of the corner of their eye
silently praying for safety
(*but they are never safe*)

the brutally powerful man-boy took his thing out of
his pants, put it in my face, rubbing it with one hand
grabbing my tiny shoulder with the other whispering
disgusting words between threats of.... *i'll kill you if you
scream.* tears slid down ten-year old cheeks as my soul
floated across the room;

...watching the innocence slip away forever...

The clacking made him stop.
The clacking pushed his member
back into dirty pants,
made the zipper slide up,
released his grip on my shoulder.
The brutally powerful man-boy
half-walked, half-ran *away;*
but not before his final threat
    of killing
      if I spoke a word.
The librarian with her high heels
saved me a minute too late.
The librarian with her high heels
saw my soul-less body;
frozen stiff in the bean bag,
liquid falling from innocent eyes.
My soul didn't want to return.
Too much damage had been done…
but little girls don't get to
choose who steals their innocence
in this powerful manly world.

Little girls who are assaulted
learn to keep it hush-hush.
No one wants to hear
what happened.
Not the librarian,
Not the police,
Not your mother,
No, not us.
Just lock it inside
    it'll go away....
There's bad men in this world.
What more do we have to say?
No need in discussing it,
or filing a report.
You are not worth the time;
besides what that boy
did to you,
it's not a crime.
Stop your damn crying
or you'll get no
ice cream
    for dessert!

Mrs.

There's something wrong with your daughter. Can you tell me what went wrong? In a few weeks' time, her weight has climbed, alarmingly high. What are you feeding her? What have you done? This little girl was so perfect, so happy, so fun. Now's she's fluffy, unhappy, and dull. Is there something you should tell us? Is there something we should know?

authoritative thoughts after a long cruel summer

The powerful man-boy
skated pass me
giving a side-ways glance.
After an instant thirty pound gain
I only resembled the girl
he'd threatened to kill.
The fat protected me
from his unforgiving eyes,
that drew me to a
moment in time;
when all innocence was loss.
As he moved slowly
the fear shook me
with the fact
that I wouldn't be
the last little girl
he would emotionally scar
during a sexual attack.

As our eyes met,
his smile grew
feeding off the fear…

all I could see
was his thing in my face,
All I could hear
were his words full of hate.

No where is safe…
no where.

seeing my attacker

He sat me down
like a child
yet spoke to me
as an adult.
His hands held
no anger
never did they
lash against
my young skin
but the words
tore open my soul
left a huge
gaping hole,
deep enough
for strangers
to see inside...
to steal what
innocence was left.

Powerful men
Protect little girls
From the brutal
Cruel world
From the savage
And the thorn
Until her bud
Is fully formed
Safe upon the sacred tree
Not abandoned
Not set free
To face the coldness,
The ruthless; alone.
No...
Men would never do that,
Not protect their daughter
Letting the thief
In their home
To steal the innocence
From between her legs
Leaving her
In a bitter world
Facing each day
With loathsome and dread.

the church bus would come
where daddy didn't live...
    anymore
but the man next door
always found a reason
to leave his wife and children
to come over and visit;
the bus would come
and I'd ride solo
in the old torn
fake leather seat
to the church
who claimed to
accept me for me
but it never did;
still, I rode alone
searching for something
or for someone
to give me a better direction
teach me discretion
to show me love

His silver tongue promises more...
With every word your desire grows...
Believing that he's an angel from God-
Delivered to deliver you from poverty;
From the complexities of living this life.

    You roll the dice,
    Betting everything
    On his sickening lies,
    That soon he'll be
    By your side,
    Leaving behind
    His lovely bride.

Dear _____,

I love you so much. I wish I was a better person so you wouldn't get so angry. Why didn't you want me to touch you? What did I do wrong? I promise to try harder to make you happy. I won't go anywhere or talk to anyone. I will not complain. I won't ask for anything. I don't have to go anywhere or do anything. We don't have to celebrate my birthday and you don't have to buy me a present. I will always love you.

_____

P.S. If you want me to go away so you never have to see me again, I will.

There's no escape
the boys surround me
in the hall
reminding me

who I am.

I am...
        fat chick
I am...
        the ugliest girl in school
I am...
        nasty, gross and disgusting
I am...
        never going to be loved
I am...
        nothing.
The eighth grade boy's
voices are silent now....
but their words
still echo in my mind.

their faces
looked happy
as the insults
rolled off their tongues
little poison daggers
piercing my soul's core.
no words
no medicine
could ever heal
the scar tissue
their taunting yielded…

middle school hallway

Seven boys encircle one girl who gained thirty pounds
after traumatic abuse, kicking her while she's down.
Where are the teachers? Not one around? Never a
friend to stick up for her? The boys are too popular.
No one cares about this fat girl! She's the punching
bag, she's the whipping post for their agitations. She's
imploding; deep within herself. The brutally cruel boys
don't realize they are only abusing her empty shell.

charna ainsworth

Every morning she's late.
She can barely convince herself to wake.
What good is facing another terrible day?

The boys will be waiting to spit their hate,
and the stupid girl dreams of moving far away.
Mom screams it's time to go,
she can't be late for work.
She blames the child for hating school;
doesn't have time to care
her daughters being abused
because she has bills to pay
and she can't be late… no, not another day.

trapped by the bodies pressed shoulder to shoulder
hovering over me eyes dancing with fire staring down
upon the girl *i used to be...*

before the eighth grade boys came around to destroy
what strands were left of me after what happened at the
public library

the shattering of my heart

When you walked into the room,
you didn't know,
when you smiled…

I was a shattered soul.

Your kindness gave me hope
that a boy could be kind,
so I replaced my fear…
     with dreams.

It was so easy to believe
you would be the one who cared.

You, were the first to kiss
the first to touch…
a glimmer of hope
in a battered world.
Slowly, I opened your hand,
presented myself;
façade in place.

You were captured…
by my spell.

Little did I know
but soon I'd see
you were the one
who captured me.

He was drunk....
    of course he was.
Why else would he be with me?
Still full of love
for his brown eyes
I sat down in the driver's seat.
His hand reached up
jerking the wheel down
crashing us beneath an oak tree.
It was the first night;
it was the first time.
he attempted to kill me.

offering a ride home

you kissed me
in the dark closet
placed your hands
upon my waist
spoke words of love
and happiness
till you were satisfied
then beckoned another
to take your place
in the darkness
where your clothes hang
that smell like you
but he doesn't

I met the boy
at seven years old
who guarded the door
so no one could
save me from a rapist
who insisted
having his way
even though I screamed no
with incredible strength

a foe in disguise of a friend

Holding me down.
Ripping fabric from my skin.
Exposing my every fear
of being used again.
Then tossed out…
no concern;
like yesterday's trash
as you search
for the next victim
who crosses your path.

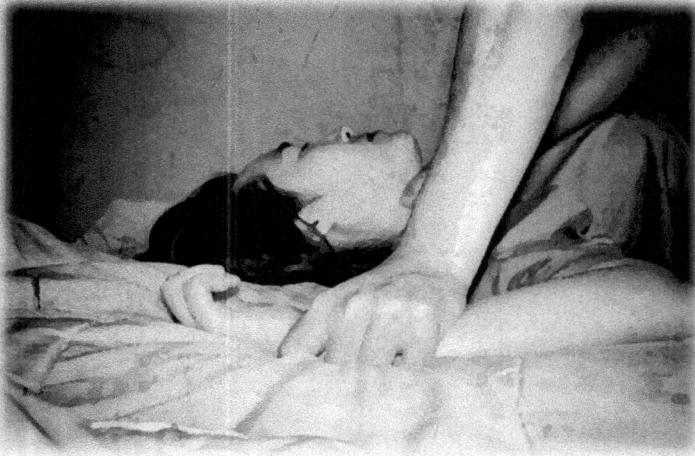

charna ainsworth

Dark shiny hair
big sultry eyes
jawline of perfection
cheekbones so high
skin, soft and tan
your face
I knew
so well.
Why did your face
turn out
to be the face
of a rapist?

a man more brutal than the rapist came home
he could have helped, should have helped the distraught girl
but his anger tore holes deeper
as he chased her out the door,
calling her a whore for being a victim of rape

Words are my only friend
Words not from your lips
Words that do not lie
Words to live by
Words I say to myself
Words a boy
would never dare
say to a girl

You are strong. You are smart. You are safe.

The boys sit in silence
writing a letter for me,
when it comes
I can't wait to read
their words of love.
In the girls bathroom stall
I open it carefully
with each word
small particles
of my soul
leave-
It says I'm nasty
the biggest skank in school
that they wouldn't
fuck me with a
monkey's dick
and to do them one last favor;
commit to suicide.

National Suicide Prevention Lifeline
1-800-273-8255

charna ainsworth

Ink on paper
Can give
Or take away
Words can ruin
Words can elevate
You're fat
You're ugly
You're a nasty skank
Wouldn't kiss you
Wouldn't fuck you…
Could ruin a girls day
…or the rest of her life.

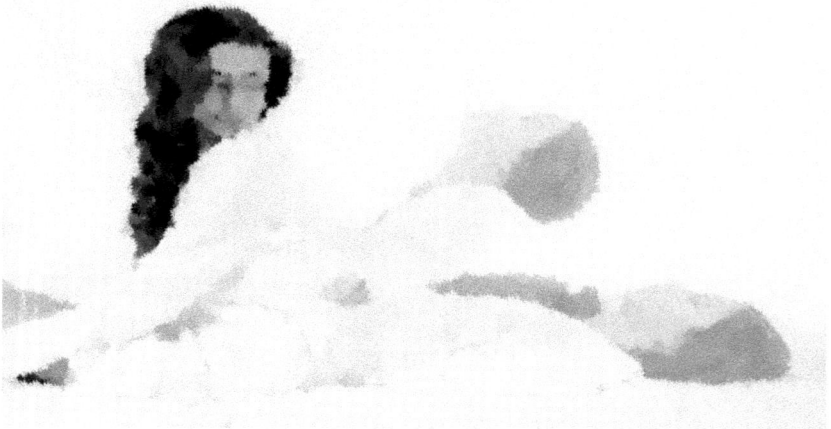

One more time
I mend my heart ♥
trying to believe
he loves me.
It's the last time
he tears it apart.
My mended heart:
    left shattered.
Time <u>doesn't</u>
heal all wounds.
What a classic
story-book lie!
My wounds
keep compiling;
they're so
high now,
I can
almost
touch the
sky.

Years; not a single touch,
no fingertips upon my skin.
Nothing could hurt me;
Then I let you in…
only by default;
pity I suppose
for your broken heart.
You touched.
You lied.
I was too cold
    to cry.
You were too busy
with every other girl
to care
if I cared.
I was blind.
Too trusting.
Not believing.
It could happen again.

first 'boyfriend'…

For the first time
lips touched my lips...

with truth,
with love.
Who could've waited
to share the news
with the entire world?
You.
I was your secret.
You hid our love
behind your girlfriend's
smile.
The kind of love
I'd waited a lifetime....
It was only a matter
of when
and I knew we would begin
a relationship to be envied.
Your eyes said it was true
no one else in the world
mattered when I was with.
.................you.

My heart had barely mended
when you stole it away
capturing the tiniest bit of hope
I had gathered in my soul.
Freely I gave you
every part of me;
so happy that you
of all people
could finally see
my true worth was endless.
Nothing had made me happier
than knowing I was your girl
until the bitter sadness
of knowing I meant nothing
when we were in public.
My heart betrayed;
the last time.
The last moment of love blindness.

It was sick; your love
    your greed
        your dirty fantasies
            tattooed on my skin.

When I'd say no
    you didn't care
        there was always rope
            laying around somewhere

It was cold
    …I asked
can I put pants on;
shoes to cover bare feet?
He didn't stop,
wouldn't stop…
sent me rolling down the street
thirty-five miles per hour.
Rolled^^^- until I landed in the ditch.
Now my beautiful skin
would be forever scarred
    because of him.

In the emergency room,
blood pooling in my skull,
ankles skinned down to the bone,
skin forever scarred
    by asphalt.
Why wasn't my life
worth one phone call
to the police?
He attempted *murder*
    on me.
Everyone who knew the truth
but didn't care;
When they did absolutely nothing;
Each and everyone
    murdered
        a piece of me.

my body lay crumbled
on the bed
unable to walk
or take a bath
because he threw
me from a moving car
tried to kill me
but it didn't work
now he sits
on the bed
needing sex
demanding sex
as the bandages
catch on the sheet
he pulls away
from my empty body

no one spoke up
no one advised me
they could all see the abuse
scabs and scars everywhere
but no one cared
they all thought
next time he does it
she'll be dead
but no one said a word
next time he'll
take it farther
no one did anything

National Domestic Violence Hotline
1-800-799-7233

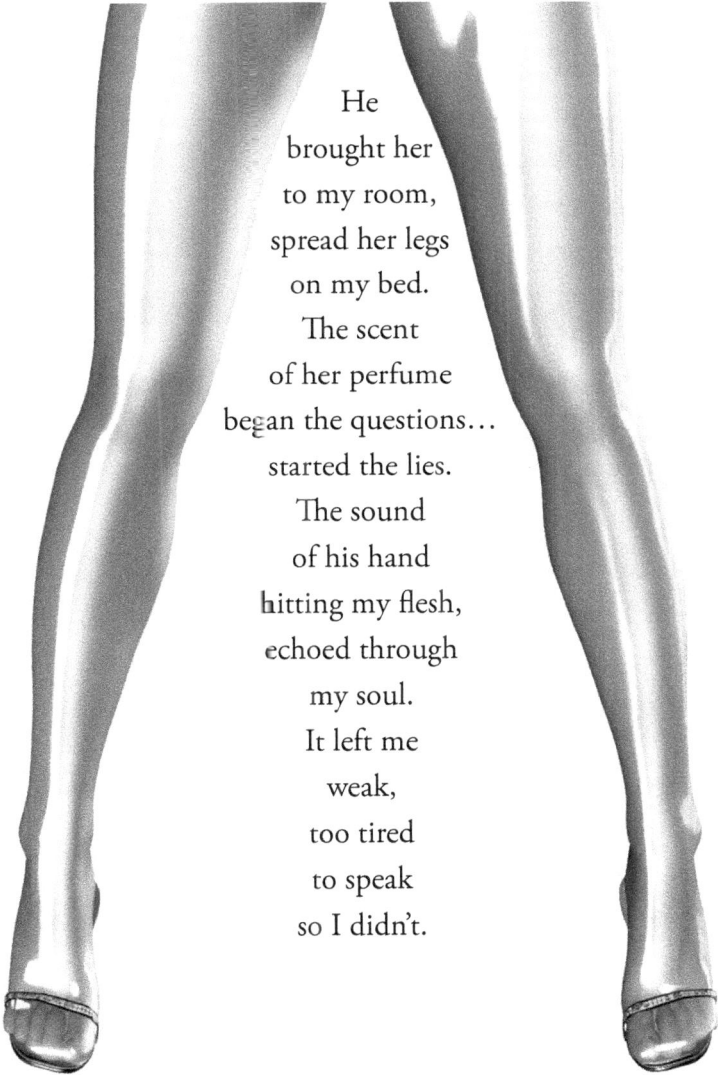

He
brought her
to my room,
spread her legs
on my bed.
The scent
of her perfume
began the questions…
started the lies.
The sound
of his hand
hitting my flesh,
echoed through
my soul.
It left me
weak,
too tired
to speak
so I didn't.

the baseball bat
made a statement
as I sat in the car
doors locked
trying to find reverse
windows smashing
being attacked
by flying glass
headlights dying
at his next swing
reverse don't fail me
I've got to get
away from here
before the bat
makes contact with me.

His hands around my throat
Smell of whiskey in the air
Lying on the cold
Hard wooden floor
Could have sworn
I was just in bed...

    Strong hands
    Picked me up
    By the neck
    Skull crashing on the floor
    Screams heard
    A quarter mile away
    Sent my savior
    To the front door...

    Why didn't he take me away?

Girls like me
Have no reason
To believe
A man
Could be kind
A man
Could be good
Just because
He is
Without a motive
Without a reason why
Because girls
Like me
Know that men
Are only good
At one thing
And that one
thing
is
goodbye...

You took advantage
of my youth…
told me this
is what I had to do
in order to get the job;
ripping my shirt
    unhooking my bra.

Biting my lip,
I swallowed the scar
you left on my soul
which no one can see.

#rosearmy

My hands held tightly
behind my back
made it so easy
for your friend
to attack.
Broad daylight
didn't matter,
assault on your mind
hungry for flesh
buttons flying
an angry exchange
left me crying…

New Orleans

Leaving you was never leaving you,
one glance over my shoulder
and you were there
watching my every move.
My debt fully paid;
I didn't owe you anything...
    not even good-bye
but you weren't satisfied
losing me so easily.
I was your meal-ticket,
your beer money,
    ...a punching bag.
No wonder it was hard for a
powerful man like you to let go.

charna ainsworth

the me too movement poetry trilogy

good girls
spread their legs wide
and shut their mouths,
unless… they are moaning
from pleasure
or faking pleasure
as they are taught to do
in order
to keep a man
Happy
to keep a man
Close
so the good girl
won't be abandoned
after the man
sees her abusive scars
that will never heal…

Pulled.............
like tug of war,
with a spineless competitor.
Dropping the rope.
Not wanting to win.
Not daring to defeat
the strong man
who said he loved me.

He put his hands around my neck.
You sat there!
(did nothing but stare
as if I didn't matter
as if you didn't care
that I'd been attacked)

sitting on a barstool

down on the dirty bathroom floor
our baby girl hides
behind a simple lock
a thin door;
drunken slurs hurled
powerful to hurt,
my arm around her tiny body
I scream internally...
never again!
when this is over,
it'll never happen
to us again

What story shall I tell the little girl who
    never speaks your name?
She remembers
    the way you yelled;
    the smell of alcohol
    on your breath everyday.
If she asks why you left
would you expect
    me to lie?

W-o-r-d-s like daggers>
P-i-e-r-c-e my soul^
From your *twisted* tongue;
Crumbled like paper...
  Tossed like trash...
  You curse under your breath.
I'm under attack.
Your h-a-t-r-e-d spills
The blood from my veins
And makes me c-r-a-v-e
A thousand pills
To ease the pain.

Out of the mouth of men...

the pursuit of survival

My eyes...
they look frightened to you
when you push me around;
but let's get this right...
after tonight
I won't be here.
There are better things
for me to do,
than beg and plea...
you'll stop abusing me.
My bags are packed.
I'm never coming back.
So don't even think about me.

careful not to repeat
the past and its defeat
I built myself up
wasn't about to be weak
when I let you in
the promises you made
Liar
when you said we'd
have a good life
Liar
your words made me
believe there were good men
Liar
it made me hopeful
that you were not a
Liar
but you are

Eyes reveal the truth,
they're windows to your soul.
Choking on three words;
simple to say…
if you mean them.

Judgement comes swift
from your perfect brain.
Always comparing
to the last woman
who shared your name.
But who am I to complain?
I deserve to be treated this way?

We could have had
A life to be jealous of
If you weren't such
A liar and a thief
Now I'm left with the
Knowledge that you're nothing
But a con-artist
And I've got to
Get away from you
Before I end up
Shot in the head
Six feet under; dead.
Why me?
There's a million
Other ladies that
Would have
Jumped in your bed.
I've had enough drama
In my life,
All I wanted was to be
A mother and wife.
Please listen when I plea...
Pack your things
And stay the hell
Away from me.

You can't stop me
from telling the
entire world the truth.
You can *hit* me.
You can *cuss* me
You can *use* me.
But it will all come back on you!

You see… boys
everything you've done to me;
The *child,* the *girl,* the *woman,*
will be placed at your feet.

Nice shoes…boy
now put 'em on
and get to steppin-

Worthy of so much more
than you had to give.
Flames silence the sounds
of your voice
that tried to drown
my dreams.
They're still alive…
and so am I.

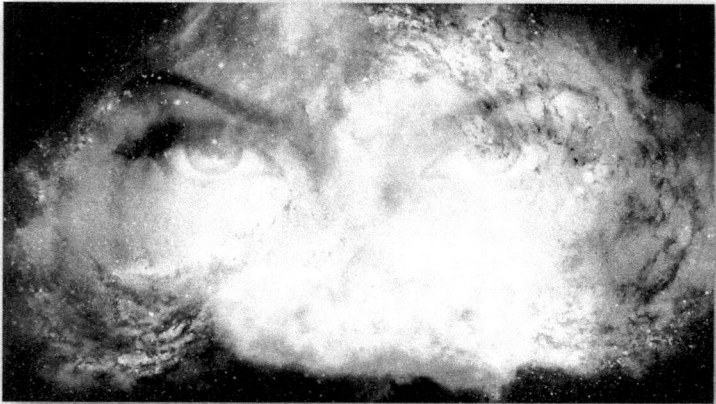

survivor

You could never see my worth.
I had to leave you in the dirt.
You made it easy to walk away,
with all the vicious words you'd say.
Never call my name again.
Hell no, we can't be friends!
And if we ever happen to meet,
just pretend you never knew me.

charna ainsworth

Trigger finger itching
Thinking of the past
When you claimed I was nothing
That I would never last
Still this pen is writing
All the words I'll never say
But maybe you'll read them
On a bright and glorious day

www.charnaainsworth.com

You thought you had me down
you thought I'd never win
but look at me now, baby
I'm back in the fight again.
They say you can't keep a
good man down;
guess they never met this woman
cause I've been grinding hard
on the hunt for your karma.

You hear our voices
getting louder…
as we say
your time is up!
No more hiding
behind closed doors.
No more knowing the truth
and looking the other way.
Now we stand together:
the power comes…
there is strength in numbers.
Our voices speak,
loud and free,
of things that
can no longer
be tolerated in
our society.

#WomenEmpowerment

It's funny you thought
my life was over
when you abandoned me,
just knew
I'd end up with nothing;
completely worthless.
Now you examine
my *comeback;*
It resembles *revenge,*
but baby, if you think
I'm thinking about you...
you better think again!

My words crush you with truth!
The way you treated me,
the things you said
and your tone of voice:
It's unacceptable!
Shameful!
Void of all dignity.

Still, I rise
out of the ashes
of your sin
and wicked lies.
Now, I know
you never knew me:
don't have a clue
of what I'm capable of.
This world doesn't
owe me anything.
And neither do you.
It's me.
I owe me
the rest of my life…
to live with dignity and truth.

#MeToo

143

Stronger

The rock by the river's edge
smoothed
by the rushing water
that moves
perpetually out to sea
that's what your
cruelness did to me.
Look; I'm smooth,
jagged edges
completely gone
telling a story
no one's ever heard
about how love
rescued me
from your sea
of profanity
and hatred.

charna ainsworth

Waves of reason crashing the fear
into tiny drops of glass
beneath my feet
that walked a
thousand miles
just to defend me
to show I'm worthy
to say I matter.
I'm not the forgotten
bruised and battered
little girl on the floor.
I fed myself poison; but I didn't die

I got stronger with each of your lies
...strong enough to walk away
    and say goodbye.

You're right where you need to be...
as far away from me
as you could get.
Good luck with your life.
Don't look over your shoulder,
I won't be here
for you to make me feel bad
or less than
because of your own choices.
You knew your opinion
topped them all;
now you are just
one of the ones
who took what you wanted
with a smile on your face,
holding the shiny knife
behind your back...
stabbing me
before walking away.

Should I apologize
for who I've become?
It was your anger,
your hate and disrespect
that challenged me
to be who I am.
I'm an independent woman
because you were....
a brutally powerful man.

Chains of madness
    kept me bound
to your belief
    that I was less
than nothing
    a welcome mat
for your dirty feet.
When you see me now
    I bet you can't believe
your words didn't destroy
    they didn't take away
the fire inside
    that'd been building
since the day you said
    I'd never have nothing
no one would ever read
    a word I'd ever
think, write or say.

Lifetimes have passed...
　　...memories collide;
unable to leave
　　the past in the past.
Your times up,
brutal man!

(who thinks he's got control,
and his power trip is totally free)

#TimesUp

charna ainsworth

It's ironic
the whole world
thinks I'm the fool
for putting up
with the horrible
things you do.
They think
I'm stupid;
just plain dumb
to not walk away
but they got it
all wrong!
It's you:
you're the broken one.
How else
could you
treat a
woman
this way?

Now you pay
for your
and your father's sins.
The reign of terror
is over and done.
    Now our daughters
    and their daughters

    will only speak of
    how it use to be,
    before women had enough
    and changed history
    to herstory.

    #herstory

charna ainsworth

Mr. Man:

Tell me why you think I'm weaker than you?
I would never disrespect another person
the way you disrespected me.

You don't own me!
I can say anything… including the word no.

breaking the silence

the purpose of resolution

charna ainsworth

Mothers…
teach your sons
to respect women.
Fathers…
teach your daughters
to *expect* respect from men.

Together, we can change
the world.

A New Vision

If I had known
I'd meet you here
during this hour,
at this specific time,
would I have prepared myself?
Knowing we could change the world?
No.
Instead of preparation
let's simply dream together…
we will let our colors blend
until the whole world is blind
to all our failures;
the things we left behind.
Then we'll begin
with a new palate;
we'll paint a new page.
Yes.
Our love will give the vision
so we are able to name our painting
'saving grace'.

charna ainsworth

Their time is up!
This has been happening
way too long.
It's time to speak!
Our voices need to be heard.
No more hiding in darkness;
Women have turned on the light.
This is the end
of fighting for
brutally powerful men
to treat us right.

I'm worthy of love and affection!
No matter what you said or what you did to me.

For a moment...
you had me
feeling like I
didn't deserve
to be heard;
wasn't worth
love and respect:
couldn't expect
true happiness.
In a flash
of your rage
I remembered
who I am...
not your possession,
my mind is free
to choose; to walk...
away so easily,
into a life
without your
sticks and
your stones:
becoming stronger
and stronger,
knowing the consequences
won't be wrong.

Seeing Clearly
She looks up, asking why?
Closes her mouth- knowing the reasons.
The door closes: no one's home.
Last day she'll lve with him.
No more!
She's done.
Never again will a man treat her this way.
She's left…
…in search of all he took away.
When she finds it;
it'll be the begirning of a new day.

letting go...
moving on...
writing a new chapter
singing a new song,
for a moment
you had me
under your thumb,
now that it's over
now that you're gone
i finally feel safe
like my life
has only just begun...

charna ainsworth

Don't for a minute think
I'm ashamed of my story,
honestly, I open the wounds
to share the words
hoping they will inspire
other women to rise above
to become so much more
than they ever thought.

reading is powerful

Out of the flames
Of desperation
From within the fire
Of your sickness
The need to control
To destroy
My confidence
Turning it to doubt
With words
With deeds
Thought you had
Me figured out
Easy to teach
I am nothing.
Little did you know
The spark you
Left behind
Reignited the fire
Making me climb
Out of the pit
Of your sick desires

Into a chair
Where queens sit.
They never allow
Men like you
A second chance
To lie and scheme
Keeping your capture
For personal gain.
No, mister
That's something
A confident queen
Would never do;
Keep company
With the likes of you.
She's realized
Her throne
And infinite worth:
It came at
A cost
But in the end
You'll get exactly
What you deserve.

dropping the mic

The strength within
gives me a name
no one has ever heard.
Going through the battles
finding my way,
triples the strong foundation.
Now no one can say
whatever they want
causing me to lay down
to be walked upon.
The part, the child
who'd been pushed around,
is standing up proud.
When you see my face;
wisdom should speak...
the words I could say.

It's been a rough road.
you should be thankful to know,
I've made it through the rain.

charna ainsworth

Your attempt to destroy
My heart
My soul
My mind
Appeared a cut and dry case,
A blow-out;
Looked just like you won...
Until I heard the voices;
They sounded
Almost like me,
Unbelievably, they survived
The worst that could be...
In an instant, I realized
That could be
Me Too.
So I gathered
Your verbal abuse
Your sexual assault
Your hatred and pain;
Gave it all to the world
And this is what they have to say...
Your time is up;
No more madness!
Time to back it up, *genius*
Quit; just go the hell away.

Peace of a ten-year olds mind
    stolen with words.
One strong touch,
but you didn't
get the best of me.
My peace remands strong.
    I made it through
the horrible memory of you
and what you did
    to try to destroy me.
Every day is a victory.
Living my life happily.

Chances are high
you're living yours in misery...
thinking of all the girls,
    of all the women
you forced yourself on;
because let's face it:
Who in heaven or hell
would want a man like you?

stupid boy
with your little brain
you should have known
I'd master the game
your shocking anger
the hostile goodbye
only left me knowing
I'd grow stronger in time
you would shrink smaller
it's the way life is
girls learn from their mistakes
stupid boys never learn
until it's too late

What a big nose
    you're peering down...
bound to get you in trouble
    one of these days.
It'll definitely be broken,
when your beady eyes see...

my life
my accomplishments
my impending future

...oh how your massive pride
    will cut you asunder,
        cause you to examine
where everything in your life
        went wrong.
What could have been...
what should have been...
if only you'd known then
what you now know
about keeping up with the Joneses
your life today
wouldn't be such a disappointment,
wouldn't feel like wasted time.

What a sick and twisted bastard
    to lie about love,
just to get what you wanted,
what you needed to survive.
Thank God, I came to my senses
while watching you leave…
with each footstep
I gathered another piece,
gluing me back together,
freeing my soul to be me.
Now, you wouldn't
recognize the woman
I've become.
Strong, successful and happy.
Like my life started over
the moment you left me.
It may surprise you to know
I don't feel sorry for you;
Your life is a disaster
of your own making
and it's sickening to see.
I guess all that shit
you piled on me
slid right back down on you.

When you see me I'll be shining
glowing with achievement,
raising up the sword
no longer silent... the abuse has stopped,
now nothing will kill the desire to share
until the whole world hears the plea;
reads the words.

No, not another girl living in fear
of any man; what he'll do or what he'll say.
It has to be different, we must find a way...
to expose these men-
put them away
as though the things they do
that ruin little girls,
that destroys a woman's mind
is a **crime.**

Words
broke the chains
that kept me bound so long.
It didn't excuse
what had been done;
it only changed
my point of view.
Now, I can see you
for exactly
who you are…
not a superstar;
no longer a villain.
You are just a human,
with fears, weaknesses
    and mental illness.

When I was little
I would have done anything
in order to make it right.
I was frightened
by your anger.
I never wanted to fight.
It was always you.
Besides; no matter
what I did,
it was never right.
Now the shoe
is on the other foot
because I'm grown
I can plainly see
    the tree
within your forest.
The one revealing
exactly who I am;
who I was supposed to be
before your cruelty
fractured me.

finding purpose

You hide in your grave
Of remorse and regret
Remembering the times
You could have been kind
Instead of dementing my soul
Into someone
I barely recognize,
Guess it made you high
Contorting love into lies.
You can't see me now
From the darkness of your grave
It would make you so mad
That I've forgiven you
And never even speak your name.
My life is my own
It's good and it's happy
And I have a beautiful home
With a family that loves me,
A career to be proud of
Even have readers who know my name.
See; all those years you tried
To kill the body and ruin my pride
In the end, it only hurt you.
I survived.

charna ainsworth

one little girl
pinned to the floor
said in a loud scream
only she heard
you have me
where you want me now
but one day i'll be big
i'll move so far away from you
you'll never see me again
then the holes you left
within my heart will begin to mend
then i'll rise up
share my story
find a family of women who care
that have been there…
together we'll rise up
put an end to the nonsense
that boys are allowed
to treat girls this way.

You thought my life was over,
my power harnessed
by your will…
It was easy
for you to think
I'd be less than nothing
after you attacked
every good thing in me
shredding my worth
for the whole world to see.
You stepped right over me
on to your next victim.
I hid in darkness;
seeking the light,
shielding my eyes
unbreaking my heart
for what seemed
like a lifetime.
Somehow I'm taller,
grown an inch or two
since you became
a loser; a failure
now that I've exposed you
and your true nature
to the world.

no more standing still
no longer hiding in the shadows
walking on your eggshells
like walking a tightrope
afraid of your anger
or what you'll do
see, I've forgotten
all about you
because I remembered me
how I'm fearfully and
wonderfully made
now you don't stand
a chance in casting your shade
while I'm shining bright
full of love, full of light.

charna ainsworth

183

By grace
I was whole
perfect; complete.
It was your evil heart
    that tore…
    that twisted me.
Imagine my life
shaped by your love…
    your devotion.
Pity is wasted,
within the reasons why;
at the turning point…
happily- waved goodbye.
Traded your trash
    for treasure.
Reaching higher
than the memory
of desertion.
No longer in need
of approval.
This is my life…
My Story.
I'll write
    the happy ending.

To: all the men and women
who thought I'd never rise
from the hate; the destruction
that's been in my life;
Surprise, surprise!
Here I am;
front cover on your newspaper
interview on your T.V.
couple of books on the shelves
for you to read.
Now I'm not bragging,
no, I'm not boasting
just wanted you to see
in the moment you had me down;
you didn't get the best of me.

movement

charna ainsworth

Dedication

Like a small storm becomes a hurricane, The Me Too Movement has become a force for change. This collection of poetry is dedicated to the people who believe the entire world deserves better. They are the ones who tirelessly work, reinventing the world day by day to become a place with less sexual harassment, assault and rape.

contents

the burden of memories

Movement

Dared to movement
by the whispers on the street
saying their time is up,
rise, stand upon your feet.
You served… you wept,
nothing was ever truly right,
close the door on the past
the future is right before your eyes.
A time is coming,
never known to man,
when women's lives matter,
our full potential finally reached,
no longer slaves to a gender
thought of as weak.
The movement has begun.

Let's Begin

stand below

catch me

if I fall

the battle rages on

we must go

it is our call

to rewrite history

in this moment

her-story

of how

of why

and who

said…

enough is enough

what's done

is done

close the books;

today we

have started

a new one…

let's begin

with chapter one

pinned beneath
the weight
of your anger
invisible shackles
against my skin
your web of lies
covering my eyes
made me easy
prey
for a day
a week
a lifetime
until
the webs
were wiped clean
by the words...
then
the shackles fell apart
from the sound
of her voice
saying
'their time is up'

poem inspired by
Oprah Winfrey's Golden Globe Speech

Hear Me Now

The masses stand together
all speaking the same thing
we want to be respected,
we want to feel safe,
we need to be believed
when we open our hearts,
something needs to change
because enough is enough.
There will be no more crying
our tears are all gone,
the power keeps building and rising
as the movement grows strong,
it encircles the globe
including every sex, color, and creed,
change is coming
as sure as I eat, live, and breathe.
Hear me now...
I said change is coming;
all we have to do is believe.

the queen has spoken
your time is up
exit to your left
exit to your right
or get on board
with the rest of the world
who says me too
my mother says…
my sister says…
my daughter says…

Now I'm standing up for them
because they would stand up for me
if I was being raped
assaulted or harassed openly
by people who have a problem
with the word no
or leave me alone
just because a woman says the words
does that mean she can be ignored?

Will You Know Me

This is the last time
you'll put your hands on me,
by mornings light
I'll be free
of your abuse, your hatred
that's so easy to see
its effect is written on my skin,
it's here in my eyes,
every time someone looks
they can see your lies...
written, etched
upon my soul
but no longer will you know me,
my heart is my own,
I will go forward,
start a new life,
create a divide so deep
your power and money
will never find me
besides...
I'd rather die
than be in your life.

In one hand, I hold the world
pushing boundaries with one tweet
just a few letters
lining up nicely
unknowingly… part of destiny.
What could happen…
no one could have told me,
I never believed
that one statement
on twitter
could bring the whole world
to hear
two words
uniting us all
survivors
victims
young or old
to complete a mission
started long ago
by a brave woman
who said come along, sister
it's time for us to move.

poem inspired by
Alyssa Milano's tweet
on October 15, 2017

Despite the Truth

You will see me rise up
to claim what is mine
with your own eyes
you will see me triumph,
ring the victory bell!
You'll see me live
a life to be proud of
even if you're in heaven
or hell.
I'll call out your name
so you can see
that I made it,
despite what you said
and how you treated me
I'll rise up and take my
rightful place…
full of mercy,
full of grace.

Invisible Bruises

If I walk into a police station
bruises on my skin
filing charges
needing protection;
because the eyes see...
action would come quickly.
If I walk into a police station
no bruises on my skin
filing charges
needing protection;
because the eyes can't see
unbelief and suspicion surround me.
His actions hurt
no more
no less
whether or not
visible marks
are there to see.

Rape Kit

When a victim
comes forward
with personal and private revelations,
it's one of the hardest things
to relive the moment,
replay details
allowing their heart, their soul
to go to the place
the time
the scar began.
They don't share their pain
for money
fortune or fame;
they share in hope
of being the last
to say metoo.

The Second Rape

Wanting to do what's right
to protect others from this pain…
lost for words
hard to explain
what happened
how he entered my body
my mind
my soul.
The nurse looks at me
as just another thing she has to do.
A blank faced doctor
without a name
examines the crime scene.
An old friend holds my hand,
not knowing what to say.
The policeman stares blankly
while making a note or two.
They all know too well
very few rapists ever get caught
and in some idiotic way
it feels like they're blaming you.

courage,
she begged for courage
to be in her heart, her soul
when she spoke his name...
the bubble burst
as the accusations
rolled from the tongue
of one so beautiful,
upon one so powerful...
it; the accusation
divided... drew a line
his side – her side
what's wrong,
many would prefer
women keep their mouths shut
like they have for centuries
but the moment has come,
now is 'the time' to speak
let the many voices of
#metoo
be heard, loud and clear.

poem inspired by
Tanushree Dutta
Indian Actress

Bringing It to Light

Believe we are making progress
as the movement moves along
it's worth the fight
it's worth the time
for our daughters
to have a better life
one that is safer
with certain rights
of protection
from men who must
learn a new way
or pay the price
for sexual abuse
for assault
that is not okay
it's not alright
we won't sweep
it under the rug
we're bringing it to light
every time another soul
reveals their truth
and says yes…
it happened to me too.

We Raised Our Hands

Our voices are heard around the world in every language,

together we are strong, speaking up for what's right,

society shifts as the movement grows

changing points of view,

it's hard to know, yet, dare I dream of all the people we may save from the pain of saying me too,

because we were brave…

we didn't remain silent…

yes, we raised our hands and said no, no more

together we are taking a stand against violence and threats

against the people who serve them like they are superior, and we are inferior,

but let me be the first to tell you

that day has passed

it lives no more.

United & Unafraid

Hungry for truth
we unite together
under one title
two words
which means so much,
a statement that adds me
to the list,
one more
in the growing numbers
of survivors
who want
to make a change
for their sisters
and brothers
because we know
things can't
go on this way,
we're too smart
to feel
our lives
don't matter.

Required Information

Help me, sir
I need to know
why am I afraid to be alone
on the street at night
or in a court room
facing the man
who almost took my life?
It would help to understand
why I feel so afraid
when the boss man
looks at me that way,
with little ones depending
on me back at home.
But what I really
need to know, sir
if you don't mind,
is why do you think
you are superior in every way,
and what do you
think is going to happen
to this world
if there isn't change?

the weight of reality

Don't Look

driving and slashing defeat
through my skin
are the words of judgment,
coming through again and again
into skin… shallow and thin
of torture endured
for too many years
where love could have saved
a fragment of who I am;
not the person you see…
weathered,
tattered,
torn,
rejected…
imprisoned by your salty sea
and blackened heart
that continually wishes evil on me,
fearing I'll never be free
and I'll never truly live
because I know
what your eyes see
when you look at me

I'm nervous
nearly all the time.
Who's to blame…
me?…
…or you?
Never enough of anything;
too much of everything.
My seams rip slowly
as your eyes roll
before the final curtain call.

Life Lessons

The sun didn't come out tomorrow
nor the next,
it clung to the horizon
refusing to truly shine
upon a wayward girl
taught to be ashamed
of needing anything
of wanting
even sunlight…
that is free.

The Mention of Your Name

Do you think
I will always
smile at you,
pretending everything
is perfectly okay?
There's no way
to justify
what you said
or what you did.
Impossible situation
you expect me
to live… in;
back against the wall
with no escape.
Planning for victory…
knowing I'll never play
your sickened games
for longer than it takes
to get the hell away
from you
and never even
mention your name –

What He Did

Out in the shadows stands a man with tear stained eyes
regretting what he said...
    what he did.
He stands all alone, no one to boss around
no place to call home;

    he weeps.
Rain begins to fall
he curses the sky or the God he never prayed to,
who would have helped.
The man strains to see a woman who use to
    share his name
and the little girl who will never be the same because of
his hatred.

Stop.
I'm tired
of living a lie.
Your words,
your promises
mean nothing...
they only ruin
and rob
what's left of
my pride.
You make yourself
out to be
a great guy
but you're
shallow and weak;
not the kind
of man I'd pick
to marry my worst enemy.

Lies and Liars

Young ears
believe every word
spoken over them
… you're stupid –
    you're fat –
    you're lazy –
no one will ever love you,
you're totally crazy.
If you think your life matters…
no one gives a damn
about a selfish little girl
that lives in the hood,
don't waste your time dreaming
you'll never amount to anything;
everybody hates you…
by tomorrow
they won't even remember
your name… _____

There's no amount of water
that will wash away
the dirtiness
I feel inside
because of the things
you said,
things you did
that scarred my soul
beyond repair
for all my days
until the end...
so I'll hide
behind the mask
you caused me to create
because of your evil ways
and live a life
looking through dim eyes
on a beautiful world
where I should have had a beautiful life.

Living in Grace

The pages are filled
with you standing
looking over my shoulder
constantly reminding me
of all my faults
and why I can't be
more like the others
with their picture – perfect lives.
Damn, now I know
you were always right.
I'm just so wrong
for needing,
for wanting,
for breathing,
and taking up precious space.
If only your words…
your lies…
would have killed,
wiped me completely
off the face…
      of earth
then you would have never
been disgraced because of me.

Twisted by Lies

Because of you I'll never have a happy childhood
I'll never truly feel safe or completely loved
for who I am…
a mess… of your making,
nothing but a tender heart

to be destroyed,
a new mind to be twisted by lies
perpetually swimming in your head
about how things would be different,
our lives wouldn't be the same… if only.
With your good witches' brew, the spell was cast
one for evil - one for good
no consequences mattered;
you had chosen…
you had walked down the path.

Cry of the Innocent

He'll do it again,
don't you know
statistics say it's not the end…
just like a hunter
he'll hunt again,
when his hands

are hungry for flesh,
when his mind
is ready for the rush
that molestation brings
from the cry of the inno-
cent
the fear in their eyes
calling out – –
but no one hears
his huge hand
covers their tiny mouth.

He's kind enough
to spare their life,
never considering the part;
the heart of them that just died.
He'll do it again,
given the time,
soon another precious child
won't escape his twisted mind.

Press Rewind

Take me to a place
where I could feel safe
the past haunts me
like a ghost
invisible to see
but always near me
influencing my each and every move.
If I could go back
to before it happened
and grow up all over again
would life still be the same?
I can't imagine it would
but oh…
how I wish it never could.

The Bottle

We reach beyond our small bedrooms
seeking shelter from reality…
for someone kind
who actually cares
what happens
when no one sees,
sometimes we find it,
most of us don't…
so, we turn to the bottle
or what's in the bottle;
anything to numb the pain,
the memories
living in our minds
day in,
day out,
of scenes,
horrible things
that should never happen
to girls like us.

Last Time

I'll go away…
so far away
you'll never have to see me again.
I found the truth in your lies,
this is the last time we'll say goodbye.

I won't miss you
that's for sure,
not even when I really need you.
Don't be sad,
don't waste your time
because I won't be here to see you cry.

A Better Life

You were wrong about me.
I do matter.
I am alive and breathing,
constantly thinking
of a better life
than you predicted.
Today looks nothing
like you said it would.
I'm normal,
happy and healthy…
while you're stuck
with the title of 'asshole'
in this world.

Who Are You?

The ringleader of your motley crew
laughed at me as you followed like puppets;
 you laughed too.
Did it make you feel special?
Did it make you feel big?
Surrounding a young girl
with little will to live,

pushing her down further than she'd ever been.
Why?
What was gained by inflicting so much pain
into a life, onto a girl
who had never even
spoken your names?

Out of Body

while you held me down
trying to steal my thunder
I was a universe away
planning my inspiring future
feeding off the pain
you inadvertently created
giving the adrenaline away
    for free
to anyone who needs
or can see themselves in me
the injected,
rejected mystery
whose life skipped a beat
when you held me down
and stole a part of me

There's a fire in my soul
it's spreading out of control
as memories of you swim...
the way you look at me,
the tone in your voice
it all makes you feel so rich
to dominate
force your will
on someone not as strong
like it's okay
to treat a woman this way
in order to boost your confidence,
believing there's no consequences
in this life or the one to come...

No Moral Compass

It's raining deep within
your twisted soul
that saw me
as nothing more
than a girl to use
in your evil mind
solely for pleasure,
another 'high'
in your simple
boring life…
no moral compass
in sight;
it's no give
only take,
it's the way
you were raised.
I look back
over my shoulder
and long
for a remake
a complete redo,
a different life…
one in which
I never met you.

Me & You

You almost had me standing at the altar willing to say I
do;
wedding gown altered, ring on my left finger
dreaming of this day like little girls do
completely enthralled with becoming one with you…

it would be perfect;
you and me against the world,
we would find a way
build our family and always stay together
which was all I ever wanted
you and me… me and you…
it was a dream come true
until she entered the room.

Across the street
behind the door
in broad daylight
a woman is assaulted
no one can hear her cry
except the man
who rips her clothes
ignoring the pleas
of stop and no,
little does he fear
the consequences
of his actions
because who will believe
this woman's word
over his?

Her Wings

Jealous of the wings
taking a bird to flight
instantly it moves… no fear in her eyes
slowly gliding on invisible wind
I watch… wishing with me she'll trade places
I could fly as far as her wings would take me

and I'd never have to face the music again
or the touch of his hand, violent and rough
the sound of his voice
his favorite word; yes
as my heart cries silently,

     no.

You are not my lover,
you are my boss,
don't look at me that way,
never say those words,
your hands shouldn't touch
nor eyes undress,
I didn't wake up
get myself ready
and drive across town for that.
All I want is to do 'my job'
and collect my pay,
my husband and I work hard
to support the family we've made,
and though you don't know this
because you've never cared enough to ask
my youngest son has been sick now
for about a year and a half.
Most days it takes all that I got
to show up and produce,
the last thing I want to deal with
is a boss who can't keep
his hands to himself...
like you.

Going Home

Walking down the street
I hear the whistle
I hear the scream
someone taunting me again.
If it's meant to be a compliment
why do I feel so afraid?
It's only sounds, it's only words,
if only I could go deaf
hit mute - press pause,
instead, I'll keep my head down
never look them in the eye,
pray I become invisible,
believe that after I pass by
no one will follow
like they did before,
wait till the coast is clear
then pick the lock on my door,
wait, I can't think about that...
not now... no, never again,
I can't remember... block it out
try and try again
to completely forget
the unforgettable.

Overdressed

The job was mine,
we had a celebration...
bought new clothes
with matching heels
because I wanted
to look my best,
to give all
I had to give
towards success.
It wasn't long
until I realized
there was only
one thing you wanted
from me.
When I didn't compromise,
didn't satisfy your needs,
I became the fired fool...
taken out with the trash.

Who would I be without the pain
of tasting the poison that lives in your veins?
Sweet, sweet, viper... disguised as love,
so desperately wanted;
temporarily blinded to the true monster in you,
hidden well behind eyes of emerald green...

remembering when I could have walked away,
saved myself a lot of pain.
Now, I wonder who would I be today...
without the pain
of speaking your name?

Tapestry of Memories

Misty memories of life before you
weave a tapestry in my mind,
of the moments when I was young…
no burdens had become
like stones weighing me down,
body was light…

soul was free
believing nothing
should befall
one so full of
life…
joy, happiness
the will to do
what the world
deems right,
until you set eyes

of darkness on me
beauty was all
I could see…
now everything good
threatens to be defiled,
if I allow these
misty memories to remain.

If a Man Gains the Whole World

Grace to forgive is mine
forgetting what was lost
knowing the risk involved
with pretending it didn't matter
cost more than I'm willing,
so with each new day
I stuff away
a little more
of the pain
that hides beneath
my thickened skin
because you touched me,
held me captive
when you could have
given me wings.
What sadness to know
how you live your life now…
full of regret;
tell me,
what did you gain
by forcing your will
while ignoring mine –

Out with the Tide

Trauma unravels pristine memories,
a simple life - waking, learning, living
no monsters under the bed
in the closet or inside my head.
Forced against the will...
unwilling to be forced,
power yielded,
escaping every day
a memory too frightful to really remember.
Wanting to go back
needing a redo
so finally, my life would be on track
and I could look like you do on Sunday mornings
so fresh, so clean
dressed in your best; smile that's obscene
to the rest of the world
whose lives haven't been a dream.
Wishing the ugliness would all go away,
go out with the tide,
never return to memory...
let me live or let me die,
it's just; I can't shake this feeling
of emptiness inside
that should have never been mine.

I Dare You

imprisoned by walls;
light secretly seeping through cracks,
only rusted chains holding me back,
truth - burns the boat;
living life on an island
surrounded by no one,
there's only me
as paper thin walls crumble,
sea salt eats rusted chains
till I break free ---
running like a river
to expose your lies,
ultimately releasing
what's left of the soul
you said you once loved -
becoming free…
forgiving the evil
no one dares to see

The One Who Trusts

grey fades to black
murky waters surround
pulling me under, pulling me down
into depths unreached by anyone before
as you take what is mine;

a thief,
one of the best
hand over my mouth
whispering words of death into young ears
that don't understand the violence, the cruelness
that can be inflicted by man upon the innocent
the virginal
the one who trusts everything will be alright
as the murky grey waters swallow her dreams
        her ambitions - her very life
...turning them to dust

there's a part
deep inside
that wants you to hurt
wants you to feel
exactly what I felt
when your hands took me
when your words raped me
rendering the vibrant young girl
a pawn, a reject,
alone
in a cold world
that doesn't care about
someone else's pain,
only their own…

The Reasons Why

My soul yearns for enough anger
to take the path of revenge.
How hard would it be
to take you down?
Certainly... I'm not your only victim
that foolishly walked into
your web of lies,
your pool of deceit...
derived from your sickened mind.

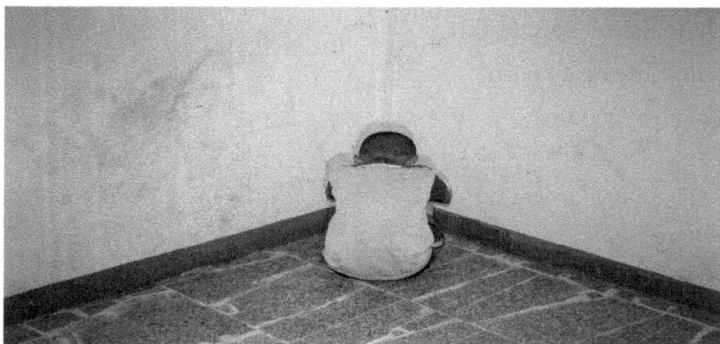

Wonder what happened to you
when you were just a boy?
Did someone treat you
the way you treated me?
If they did...
would it make it easier
for me to forgive or forget?

In the End

The hunger to strike back
to make you pay
seems overwhelming
especially today
when I'm afraid
to go out alone
because of what happened to me.
It's been three years now
but all I can see
is your face in my face,
your breath on my skin,
threatening to kill me
and my family
if I said a single word.
I'm saying it now
and even though
it may be wrong,
I'm praying
in the end
you'll get
what you deserve.

Whiskey and Cigarettes

Three o'clock in the morning
I stare at the wall
seeing your face again,
the nightmare returns,
I smell your breath…
whiskey and cigarettes,
hear the pounding of my head against the wooden floor
as your hands grip tighter
against my throat.

Tell me;
do you think that's love?
Rotting away
in a jail cell
is the only place you should be.
Instead, you're out
running free…
searching for your next victim
rest assured,

it won't be me.

What Could Have Been

Below the surface
under the layers of skin
are trapped voices
repeating their sin
producing invisible scars
no one can see
yet everyone can sense
ten steps away from me.
There's something missing
from my eyes
not one single soul
can pretend or deny
should have been mine.

the promise of change

Ounce of Happiness

I'm leaving…

and you don't even know,
you can't even see I've packed my bags
everything I own
in the corners of my mind
leaving on the day I find half a chance
to forget this place
so dry… so cold
for a soul like mine to find rest
an ounce of happiness;
oh, what's the use
of cleaning what's dirty
of what's used…
time to search for someplace new
to call home sweet home.

Twisted Rules

Inside the mind
within the game
you played so well,
such twisted rules
of what you wanted
me to be
what you wanted
me to see
about who you touched with love...
who was touched in anger,
always hiding behind
those dark eyes
that shed tears
when no eyes could see
how tormented your soul
became
as your throne
slowly slipped away...
all because
I escaped
and wrote the words.

charna ainsworth

To Find Grace

In the room
of darkness and light
beyond the locked door
inside of the child
within a small heart
lives a soul…
it never forgets what happened,
it always remembers your face,
whenever evil came calling
the little girl
knelt to the floor
to find grace…

Eyes of blue

followed
daring
words
to stumble
from a
tight-lipped
mouth
frozen
by
self-doubt
believing lies
of never
being enough.
Now the
blue faded…
grey
is all that's
left behind.
The words
are still unspoken
yet written
releasing
the past.

All the Words You Never Said

The moment you flipped
the image around
to shield your eyes
from the only beauty
I'd ever found
was the moment our final goodbye
began to take shape, began to take root.
Each new leaf, it grows
from the plethora of your rudeness…
the days you're unkind
when you roll your eyes at my presence
the moments you separate your life
from mine.
When we were supposed to be
…for forever
…now we don't have a single day
to treasure our life together.
One day you'll regret
all the words
you never said
but I won't waste
another second on you;
I'll be enjoying happiness
somewhere… far away –

One day soon
you'll never see me again.
I'll be out of your reach
too far to hold
too far to touch
too far to hear
too far to regret
all the nasty
things you did
that sent me
… away.
Live with it, baby.
You tossed
the love of your life
…away,
like nothing,
like garbage,
with your hate
your lies.
Now, I'm stronger
I don't need you…
just go swim
in your own righteousness
and wave goodbye –

True Reflection

with words
you clipped my wings
grounding me
to no longer fly;
with hate
you stole my voice
leaving me
with nothing to say;
for too long
I lived this way...
then one day
my wings began to grow
my mouth began to speak;
I look down
upon you,
so small
insignificant and weak,
whispering a prayer...
you'd gaze
at yourself
in a mirror
and finally see
in yourself
what you did to me.

Perfect & Justified

What you did in darkness
has found its way
into the light,
no more a secret
your deeds
will be known
by the world.
How does it feel
to be on a pedestal
all alone
perfect and justified
in your hate crimes
against a woman
who you promised
to love and cherish?

Eat and Be Full

When you pushed me down
I rose again,
then you slandered my name
but I prevailed.
You looked at me...
labeling me as weak;
the weakness changed
to strength
because of the heartbreak
caused by your lies.
Now, I am no longer
the one who cries
for mercy.
It's a cycle...
a seed,
a sprout,
a tree...
yielding its fruit.
Eat and be full, Mister:
Devour what you've produced.

My Good Vibe

Mere days…
created a gulf
of before and after,
the reference point
clearly defined
by physical changes
plain to see
by anyone who cared,
even by those who didn't…
that fear
had a grip on me.
I was so alone,
no protection,
no shoulder to lean on…
'the aftermath'
ruled my life,
blurred my vision,
stole my good vibe,
right until the moment
I screamed, "No more! –
This is my life."

Don't you know someday you'll pay for your sins
what you did… the entire universe will know
every ugly deed, every cruel word you said
it will not be hidden,
each and every soul will be cleansed
    …in the end.
When the Lord asks, did you learn to love?
I will answer… yes,
despite the pain

despite the trials
despite the lies
I loved;
I forgave…
and I reached out
to help the next
person up.

   What will you say?

Love Me for Me

Show me who you are
don't cover up the past
I need to know
if we're going to make this last
beyond a first date
beyond a first kiss
I need to know
what you stand for
how you'll treat me
and my kids
because in my mind
I dream I will find
a man who can love me
and my children freely…
a man who would hold his tongue
reveal his heart
and never lay a finger on me.

In the Driver's Seat

You think I'm lost
can't make it on my own
need a strong man
to hold my hand,
let me tell you something...
right here, right now...
you've got me all wrong;
I'm not a damsel in distress,
not looking for a knight
in shining armor...
No, I know where I'm going
and I got what it takes,
don't need a man
to deliver my fate.
I'm in the driver's seat,
I can make it on my own.
You might think I'm running scared
but I'm running this one
all the way to home.

Born to Bloom

Integrity carry me
beyond your expectations
of what I can accomplish
with every day.
I'll push away
the world's definition
of who I'm supposed to be
and what I'm supposed to do
because I believe
all flowers are born
...to bloom.

A Friend of Mine

The strength God gave you
the muscle to hold me down
means nothing to me now
because I no longer hide in silence
never speaking of what you did,
it doesn't bother me
if the whole world knows,
I didn't do anything wrong
I didn't ask to be assaulted,
you know I thought you were
a friend of mine,
not a rapist.

What Will You Say

Get out of my face
don't say that to me
you don't know
who you're talking to,
I won't give up that easily.
You think you'll destroy
my heart of gold,
even though it cracks
you can't break the mold.
I was born to do great things
and this you will never change
with your nasty words of hate.
At the end of your life,
on judgment day
what will you say…

The Flame

Wings flutter
cause and effect
words spoken
only time can heal,
wasted energy…
spit in my eye,
little girls believing
little boys believing
a different system
is woven out of the stories
how the victims survived
and revised the words
till their glory came alive
and ignited the flame
glowing in their eyes,
not for power,
for change…
for life.

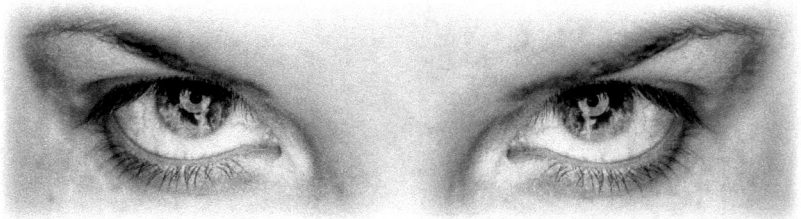

Heart of Hearts

If you think it's okay
to have your way
with any person
you want to touch
you're dead wrong,
even if it's what
you learned
as a little boy
lying in your bed
praying to fall asleep
before those big hands
reached out
touching you in places
they shouldn't be;
as a man you can choose
a different path
you can break the chain;
somewhere in
your heart of hearts
you know
it's a crime
it's wrong
you don't have
to live that way.

Easier Than it Seems

When I say no,
listen.
When I say stop,
do it.
You can control
yourself,
you are not
a beast,
we are both
human,
making choices
every day.
When I choose
to kiss you
it doesn't mean
I want to go
all the way.

You think I don't remember; you think I'll forget,

the way you ripped my dress, the way you pulled my hair.

Let me tell you something... that will stay on your mind...

I'll never forget what you did!

Every day I'll wake up and fight for what's right.

Every day you wake up... I hope you feel afraid... because I'm still alive.

I won't give up or give out until the whole world knows

that what you did to me... is a crime.

One you should have to repay with your precious time.

Powerful Ammunition

There is no guilt
    no shame
I didn't do no wrong
don't need any alibi
or testament of character
no judge to convict me
no jury to review evidence
when the world looks at me
a victim of sexual violence
is all they can see
but there's so much more
to me than that,
I'm a survivor of your sin,
ammunition against the next man
who thinks my eyes will go blind
when he uses his hands
to commit another crime,
stealing her peace of mind
and precious innocence.

Mercy's Way

Looking over my shoulder,
it's a long way down
from where I come.
Shadows follow close behind
reminding me of the times
I had no one to call friend.
Climbing higher,
I realized
the moment I settled
for less
than what is deserved.
The test…
didn't pass,
so, it presented
again, and again,
allowing me to suffer
    to grow
    to win.

Watch me now as I rise
and you fall
all because of this game called life.
I win -- you lose...
each step I take... like a thousand miles
away from you -
filled with hate,
me; with hope,
selective memory can be mine,
rise above it, never look back
until my future barely resembles
    my past.

Live Each Moment

It was never my fault
never me to blame
why carry the sorrow
why covered with shame
over something I didn't do,
would never do
to another person
to another soul,
I'll carry these burdens
down to the grave
but I tire of them weighing me down
so they're lifted off my shoulders
as of today,
my eyes won't speak
of sadness…
they will say I'm wise,
my heart won't live
in memories
it will focus on today
then I can live each moment
for the rest of my life with happiness,
on purpose…
letting love be my guide.

A Perfect Rain

It's a new life for me,
closing the door on yesterday,
my old ways
can't haunt me,
not another day.
I'm free
from the way things
used to be…
full of passion
for what's to come,
the new person
I'll soon see
staring back at me
from every angle
in every mirror
from this day forward.
Just a moment
to release these chains,
watch them rust
in a perfect rain,
full of promise
bringing change and peace.

Undefined

This act will not
define my life,
the cruelty can't
have my future,
it's ugliness
will never ruin
the beauty I'll gain
or the compassion
that grows
for women
who've experienced
the same
treatment from the
hands of a man
hell-bent on power,
blind to the crimes
he's committed
time and again,
that will never be erased
just left... undefined
no rhyme, no reason,
simply left behind
so I can get on
with my life.

Crushed Intentions

The flowers smell sweeter
because I survived,
the sunset is richer
in my eyes,
you had me down...
could have taken my life...
but you didn't;
I survived...
to celebrate a life
well – lived,
to have a family...
loving kids,
wonderful husband,
a beautiful house.
See, you didn't destroy me
... only yourself.

Protect Yourself

Advice for the teenager
who will probably pretend
she's not interested...
learn to protect yourself
where ever you are
whomever you're with,
you can become a statistic
in a matter of minutes,
don't ignore that
sinking feeling down in your gut...
if a person or place feels unsafe
don't be polite... run for your life.

1988

The pleasure is knowing there was no success in your attempt to end my happiness.

You didn't win.

I still smile and laugh sometimes… in spite of what you did.

A Perfect Guy

Been blindsided,
shocked by your hate.
When you said
you loved me
I believed
without hesitation.
Fate has a funny way…
it'll even the score.
You should watch your back,
because before you know what's happening
you will be the one to lose it all,
everything so important to you,
all for your foolish pride
but hey…
you're a perfect guy.
You'll always have
a perfect life…

Never Say My Name Again

You see me as shallow and weak
thinking you have power over me
you twist and turn
every word... every sound
until my broken will
comes tumbling down
into your hand
which reaches out
to push my pride aside
    -    but not today.
Today, I'll stand my ground,
today, I won't be pushed around
that was the last time
you'll say my name,
the last time I'll feel the pain
of your hands touching my body
where they shouldn't be.
Today will be the end
of you abusing me.

Better Than Qualified

Stronger each minute
you're not around
reminding me
I'm just a girl,
a weakling,
can't do anything right...
according to you
I should just die
but I'm here to tell you
that just ain't the case,
cause my daddy didn't raise no fool,
I'm better than qualified
to kick your ass
while blowing you a kiss goodbye,
then on the day
you realize what you lost,
don't come crying to me
because I'll be long gone.

Karma's Day

One day you'll see me
in a different light,
you'll hardly recognize
the girl you knew before,
I'll be the woman
with a confident smile,
without worry in her eyes
there… sitting on top of the world,
you will look up to see
all your bullying…
all the harsh words…
had no lasting effect on me,
they rolled off,
    rolled down…
soaked the ground
where you now stand;
even way back then
I knew I'd never
want to be in your shoes,
when the way
you treated me
came back around to you.

So Have I

Are you jealous of the way I shine?
It was your sickened deeds
that put my heart on the line
causing me to swim
least I die
from the poison you injected
growing stronger over time
like a seed
sown in rich soil
that grows a strong vine;
it threatens to kill the tree...
thorns dig deeper
into tender bark,
yet... it refuses to die,
the tree grows thicker skin
and so have I;
it was the only way
to make it through this life.

A Life Meant for Good

Look at me
with new eyes,
ones that see me
as part of you
connected by the creator
of everything good…
would you be so evil to me,
if it meant you were
being evil to yourself
or to God?
This is why
the pain you caused
by your evil ways
cannot stay in my life…
a life meant for good.
You took enough;
I draw the line,
not one more day
will your evil deeds
cross my mind.

You Are the Flower

Yellow flowers softly swaying
in a gentle wind,
only wanting to be admired.
Pick them one by one,
place them in a beautiful vase
to enjoy them again.
Beautiful flowers rise up
to decorate the day.
It's only natural
to pick one or two…
giving them to someone you love.
Imagine; you are the flower.
Everyone can see
your beautiful colors…
shiny and carefree.
He picks you from the field,
displays you to the world,
then secretly poisons
your heart and soul
with his deeds and words.
Tell me…
  is that love?

There's no stopping me,
you will never win,
no matter what you did...
I will rise and rise again,
higher than you've ever been
or could ever be,
I'll have a happy life...
just you wait and see.

the reward of perseverance

Renewed

out in the distance
there's a place to call home
where the memories
can't be remembered
and the past lets go
so I can move on…
working and searching,
I want to move forward
to the life that's ahead
where wounds and holes
heal completely
till they are gone
and I'll never
have to deal with
them again

No Proclamation

The power you steal
with strong hands
and nasty words
was mine
not yours,
and I'm taking it back.
That power is mine
to live this life
the best I can
to protect the innocent
to share my wisdom
by speaking the truth
of what people do
behind closed doors
when they think
no one will ever know...
I will know
and I will tell
of their dark deeds
until all women
are strong enough
to fight back
and say the word 'no'.

The Women of Your Life

God did not give man
his power and strength
to use it on women and girls
in brutally simplistic ways.
Men were given enough power
of their own; needn't become thieves
to feel superior in a world
driven by strength-
Your time is up!
Say goodbye to the way things have been
women are rising up ^
taking a new position,
a death grip stance
that 'this' has to end.
Don't be alarmed when we receive equal pay
or the job position you thought you had...
because enough is enough
it's time to look at the other half
and remember who we are...
your mothers, your wives,
your sisters, your daughters.
Bottom line:
We deserve respect.

Sisterhood

Smothered… I'm coming up for air
joining the movement that says I matter
to someone in this world.
I'm not just a girl to be used or abused
for pleasure or gain.
They say there's strength to be had,

with greater numbers there is power for the powerless
for the weakened, for the woman who needs someone,
anyone to notice she's alive…
an unbelievable miracle
in the flesh.

Open the Debate

Colliding powers
stop the press
get off the train
find your way
pick up your feet
join the crowd
the truth is free,
a movement for sure
to celebrate
a movement for us
to open the debate
of what's right
and what's wrong,
the decades have flown
women have grown
now it's time
men noticed
the change.

The Beginning of the End

The birth of a new day is coming
there's pain in the delivery
minds are open
secrets revealed
lives lay shattered
triumph is lived
by the survivors,
predators feel shame,
no one wants
to say me too...
let a new day begin.

A New Generation

whatever it takes to change the world
to open the eyes of the ones in charge
rewrite the laws
today is the day
it's past time
hear our voices,
we've grown weary
of the way
women are treated...
it's time to raise our standards,
begin a new chapter in world history
teach our children
when they are babies
then a new generation
will rise up
out of the ashes of disrespect
changing our world
into a much safer place

Call You Out by Name

My arms surround the children if only in my mind
to protect them from the monsters that lurk in the night
pulling women, girls, and boys into darkened rooms
with the power of their voices,
taking pleasure in what they do.
I won't be ashamed when I call you out by name,
I won't blink an eye when judgment is passed on your life,

the way I see it... if you did it to them - you did it to me.
Most of your kind will never face a judge so I'll take the
victory as if it's my own,
believing it could protect one more woman, girl or boy
    when it's all said and done.

Manners

What if I write these words
and my daughters are never
sexually assaulted?

If I tell the stories,
as difficult as it is,
could it change their future?

When I stand up
and shout me too,
will it change their legacy?

Imagine if I sat silently,
legs crossed
and never opened
my mouth;
like I'm supposed to?

Call it Like it Is

Call out your pig
a French lady says,
say his name
to all the world
now they know
he's been harassing
you for sex,
his singular pleasure,
most likely you are
not his only victim…
that's for sure.
The French lady laughs
as she learns I'm appalled
with the words she used,
call it like it is…
if he was a fox
we'd never call him a pig.

poem inspired by
Peggy Sastre
French Philosopher
Co-Author of the Le Monde Letter

Like It or Not

Waiting for the shift
when is it going to begin?
Look… at last
I think it's here,
look how far we've come.
A hundred years ago
women received the right to vote,
still, we dream for more…
believing it's only right
to decide for ourselves
if we want
a man's affections
or not –
it should always have been our choice
and we want our voices to be heard
and respected,
    -   like it or not.

#metooers

Let the victory pour out
we're winning the war
making the workplace safer
much more transparent
with everything we do
because we're not going to sit idly by
allowing brutally powerful men,
to steal our thunder
their time is up,
I'll say it again,
their time is up
and I'll never stop saying it until
the whole world knows they are not alone.
It happened to me,
it happened to you,
now let's band together and show
the brutally powerful man
what #metooers can do.

At What Cost

Listen to our voices
they want to be heard
we'll whisper
we'll scream
we won't be turned away
until it is clear
we'll take no more
of your little happy pills,
see, you can't get cheap thrills
at the expense of our souls
leaving us used and abused
by dirty old men
    like you –

See the Words

Running swiftly past a burning book
wishing it didn't contain my name,
needing the rain to fall…
to hear a voice,
that sets me free from the memories -
holding me down…

chained to a past
that refuses to let go,
smells of sweat,
words I'll never forget,
wounds that never heal.
Only now,
I see hope

every time I hear
a voice say
or see the words…
me too.
It frees me from being alone; from suffering in silence
because of the violence I've known…
one day I'm going to break free,
bury these memories
let the rain wash away the pain
then live life on purpose.

50 – 50

It's been too long coming
rumbling like a distant train
plenty of power
plenty of know how
to complete the job.
Once and for all
our voices will be heard.
The scales are even!
Fifty percent men
fifty percent women
make up the population
of our world.
If you think calling for an end
is too much to ask
wait until you hold
your baby daughter
in your arms
knowing she will grow up
in the same situation
unless we take a stand
against sexual violence and harassment.

The Interview

Pardon me sir, are you a rapist?
I need to know before we talk.
Didn't mean to offend
but we can't be friends
until I know the truth.
Tell me, do you molest
or have you been molested?
There are children at home
and I don't mean to
sound like a police inspector
but I'm their only protector.
Certainly, we can see eye to eye
at some point every woman
ask these kinds of questions,
and I really need to know the answers.
Have you ever been charged
of committing a sexual crime?
Now look, there is no reason
to get so incredibly mad;
I'm only being smart before I get in that cab
that will take us to a place where we'll be alone.
If you're not willing
to talk about the real you,
it's time for me to go home.

Mother May I

Shocking to believe…studies show up to seventy percent of women will experience sexual violence in their lifetime.

This means we are not alone.

Violence against women must end. We're strong enough to change the laws,

rewrite the rules, make this world a safer place

at our colleges, at our schools.

We can make a change.

It starts in your home with your child… boy or girl.

You are the teacher, you can be the difference, together, mothers can change the world.

With each person
who says me too,
the walls crumble
un-shielding the guilty
opening our eyes
to the truth.
Sex offenders
do not discriminate;
all ages
all sexes
all colors
and religions
are affected.
With the number of
women growing,
unafraid to say it happened
to them too…
our voices
are being heard
around the world…

Two Words

One day in the future young girls are going to read
about what one woman started
about how she believed…
that two little words could identify and collect

women in a new way in which the world would never forget.
We have one thing in common that unites us all,
making the women of the world a very powerful source,
potential energy to pursue change
all… asking for one simple thing:
R-E-S-P-E-C-T
-respect my decisions
-respect my personal boundaries
-respect me (.) period

poem inspired by
Tarana Burke
Founder of the Me Too movement

Powerful

It will be your eyes
that will see
my success
you'll witness
my happiness
with shock
and amazement.
You will question
in your savage mine
how I could prosper
after all you
said and did
to destroy my life;
my confidence.
Deep inside
my wounded heart,
the child in me
will look in your eyes
and smile
reminding you…
'I'm still alive.'

'the' metoo movement

Tarana Burke worked diligently for ten years.

Alyssa Milano tweeted a call to survivors...

...so the whole world could sense the magnitude of #me-too.

Two words, stating: I have been sexually assaulted or harassed.

In twenty-four hours: half a million tweets followed... hashtag me too had finally bloomed.

America Ferrera, Lady Gaga, Debra Messing and Katie Couric answered,

to name a few -

within forty-eight hours 'the' movement picked up steam;

twelve million posts, comments and tweets.

There's strength in numbers.

We have something to say.

Listen!

Beloved reader,

You are the reason I write. *You*... and every soul who is searching for something... anything to read that tells them they are not alone. With every poem, with each line, I poured out my heart. Your eyes read moments of life: some ugly, some beautiful. Only you can decide their meaning. Thank you for taking time and allowing yourself the journey of Movement. Please know you are appreciated more than you could ever imagine. Without *you* and your love for poetry, there would be no reason for me to write another line. If you find even a small part of yourself in these pages, every moment of revealing my heart will become meaningful.

about the poet -

Charna Ainsworth is a novelist and an award-winning poet. She lives in South Mississippi, outside of a small southern town with her family.

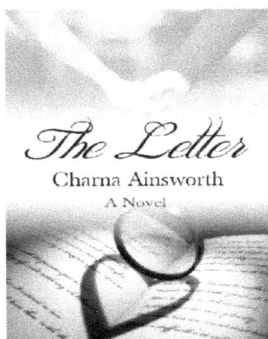

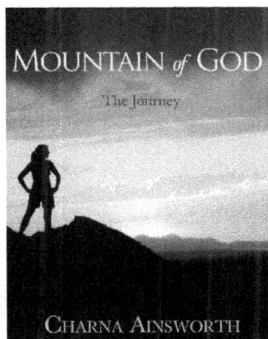

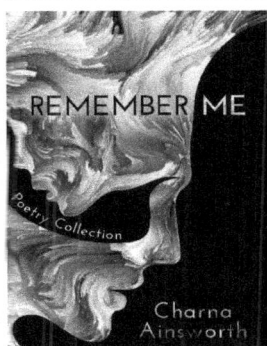

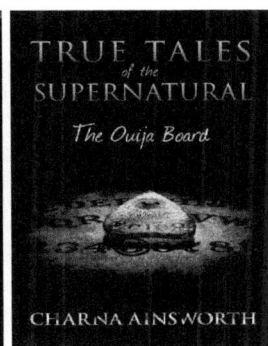

More Great Books by Charna Ainsworth

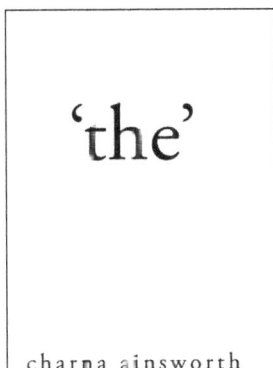

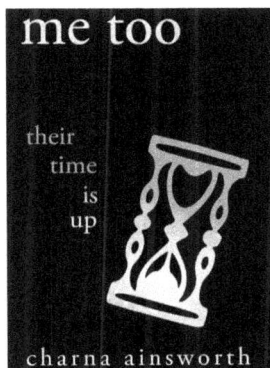

www.charnaainsworth.com

What's coming next?

Sol-See

THE SQUIRREL GIRL

MARIA AINSWORTH

Reviews are welcomed and appreciated. Links to multiple book venues are located at: www.charnaainsworth.com